Beautiful Doodles

Nellie Ryan

First published in Great Britain in 2007 by Buster Books,
an imprint of Michael O'Mara Books Limited,
9 Lion Yard, Tremadoc Road,
London SW4 7NQ

A CIP catalogue record for this book is available from the British Library.

ISBN: 978-1-905158-94-2

10 9 8 7 6 5

Illustrated by Nellie Ryan for Charlotte and Sophie
Edited by Ellen Bailey
Designed by Zoe Quayle
Printed and bound in Malaysia

www.mombooks.com/busterbooks

Furnish the doll's house.

Fill the frames.

Decorate the fan.

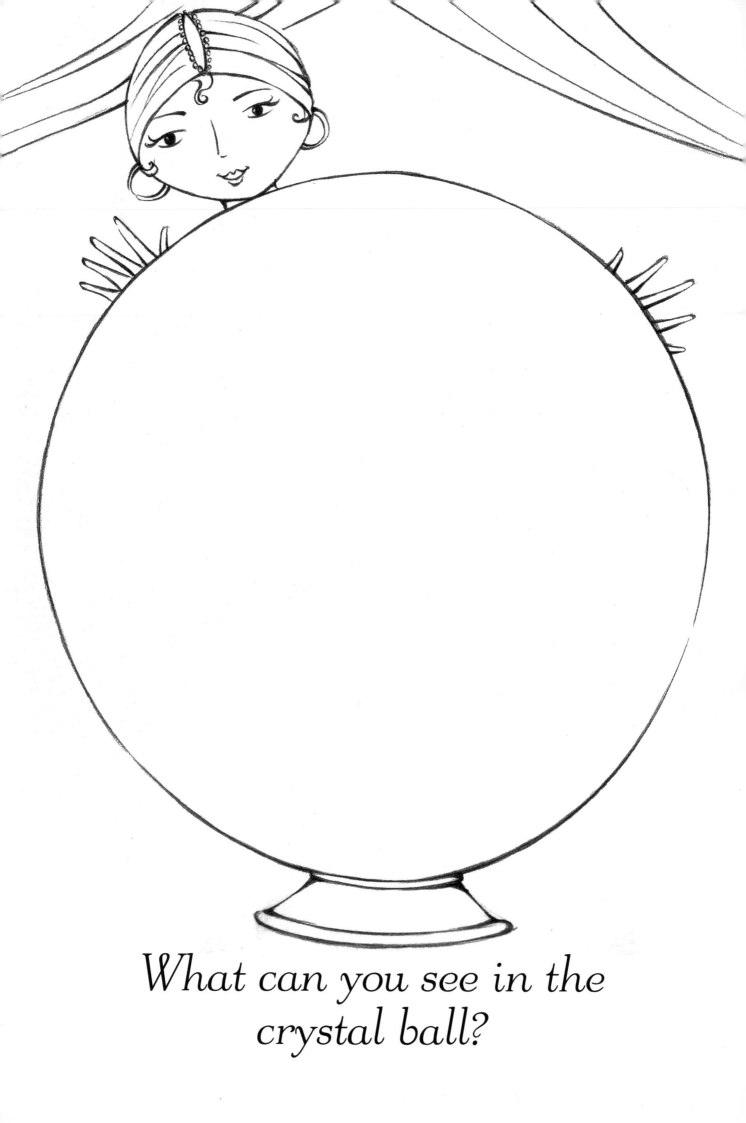

What can you see in the
crystal ball?

Decorate the paper-doll's clothes.

What animals are in the pet shop?

What have you baked?

Bubbles everywhere!

Finish the dandelions.

Decorate the piggy bank.

What beautiful jewellery!

What can you see out
of the window?

Hundreds of flowers.

Decorate the crowns.

Give the butterflies beautiful wings.

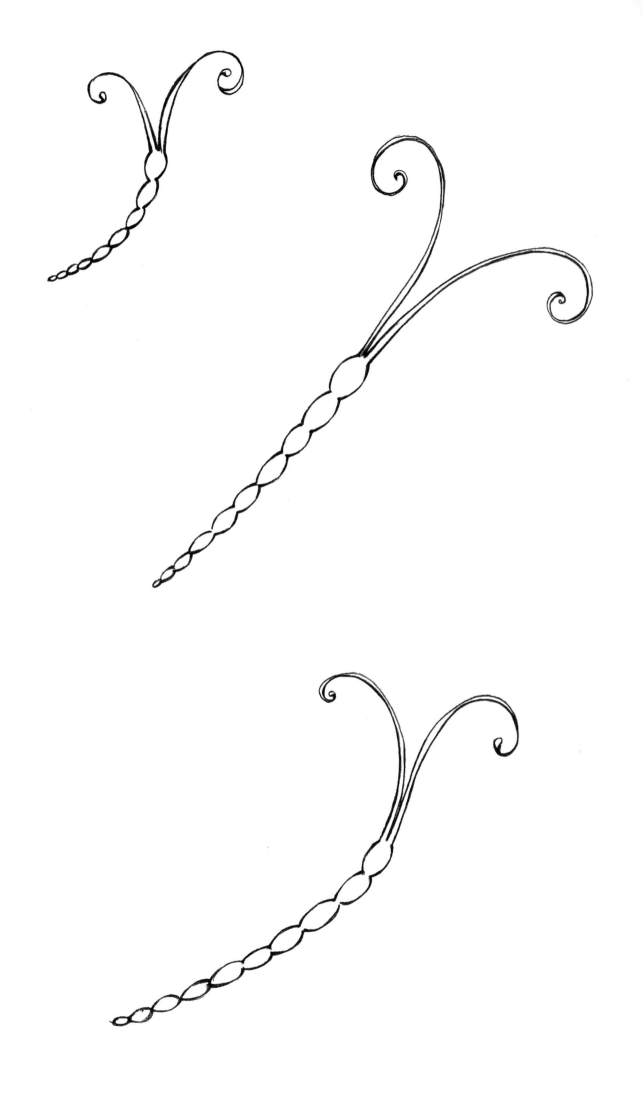

Customize your car.

Decorate the masks.

Arrange flowers in these vases.

*Give me glamorous sunglasses
and earrings.*

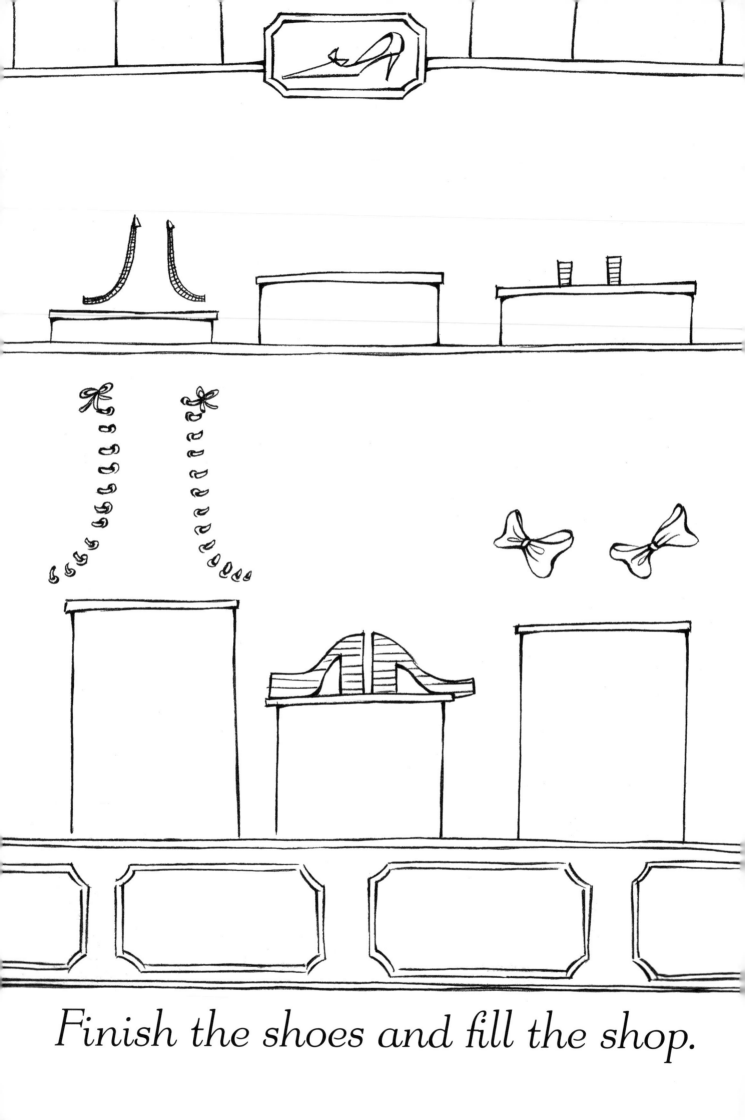

Finish the shoes and fill the shop.

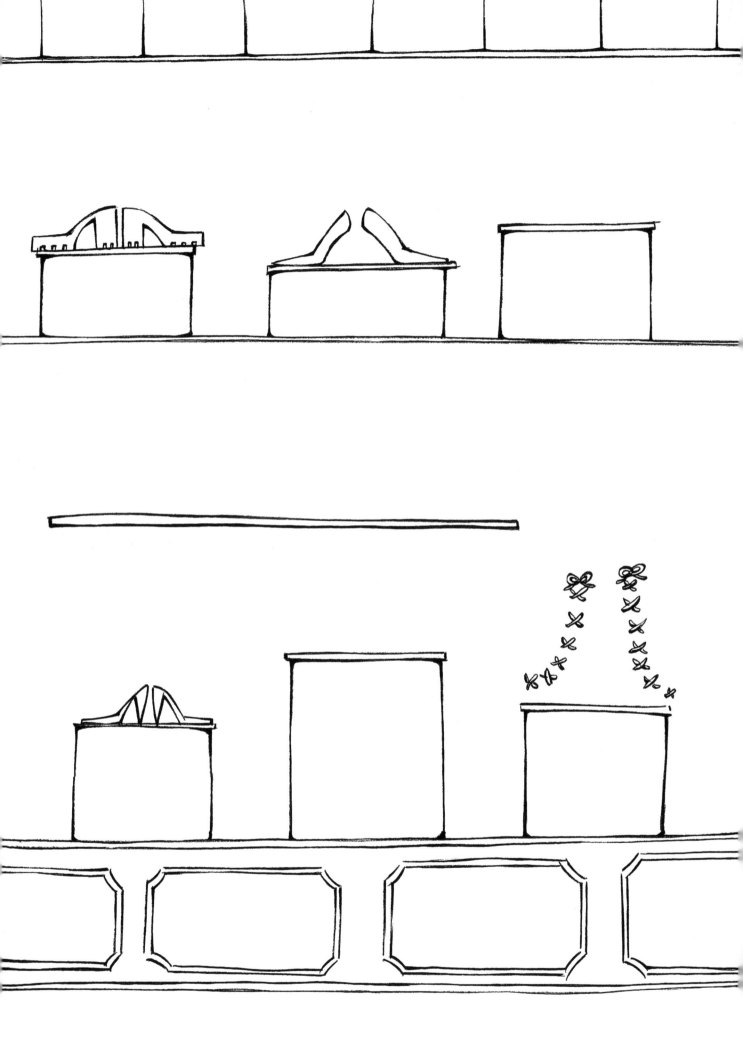

What kinds of chocolates are in the box?

Washday

Decorate the cupcakes.

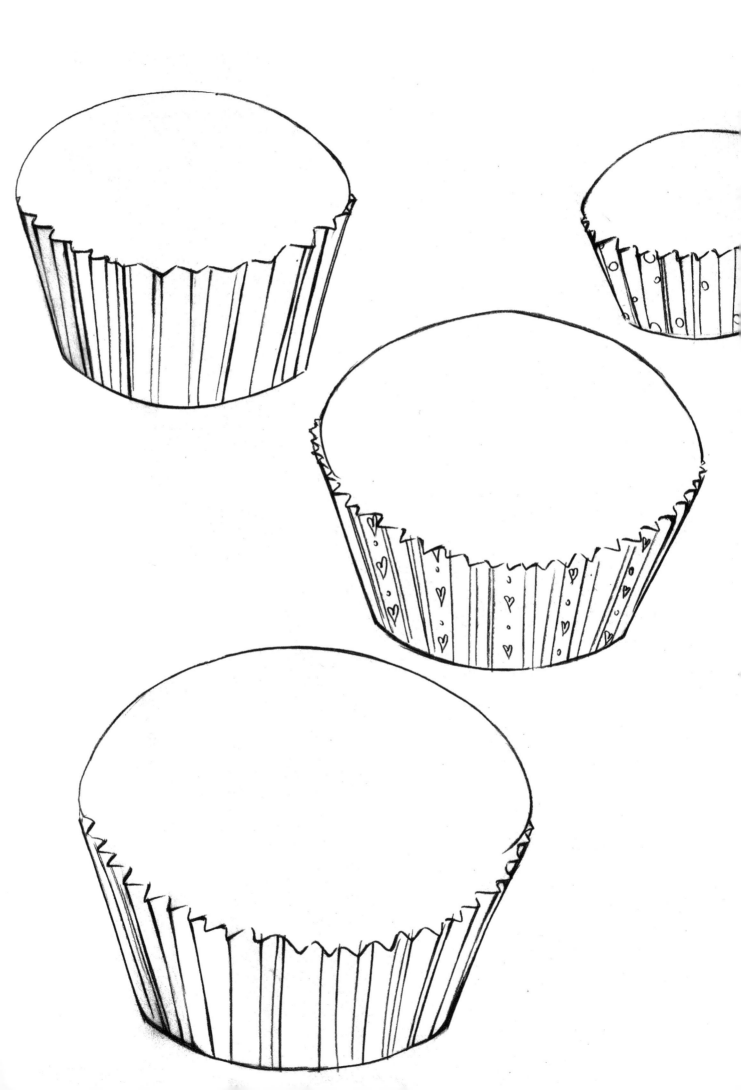

A fashionista's wardrobe.

Give the dog a designer outfit.

What can you conjure
out of the hat?

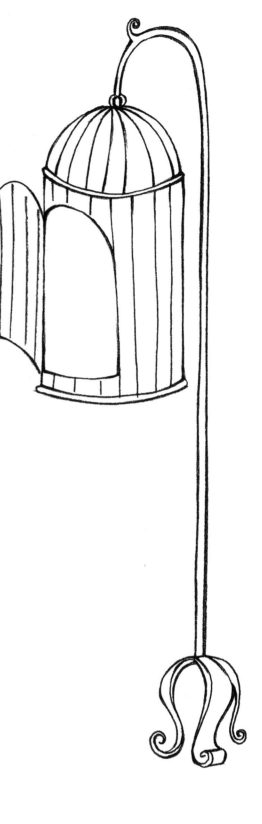

Oh no – the birds have escaped!

What can you see through the telescope?

Noodles – yum!

Where has the magic
carpet taken you?

Mix up a love potion.

Give us glamorous hairstyles.

Paint a masterpiece.

Snowflakes are falling!

What is on these badges?

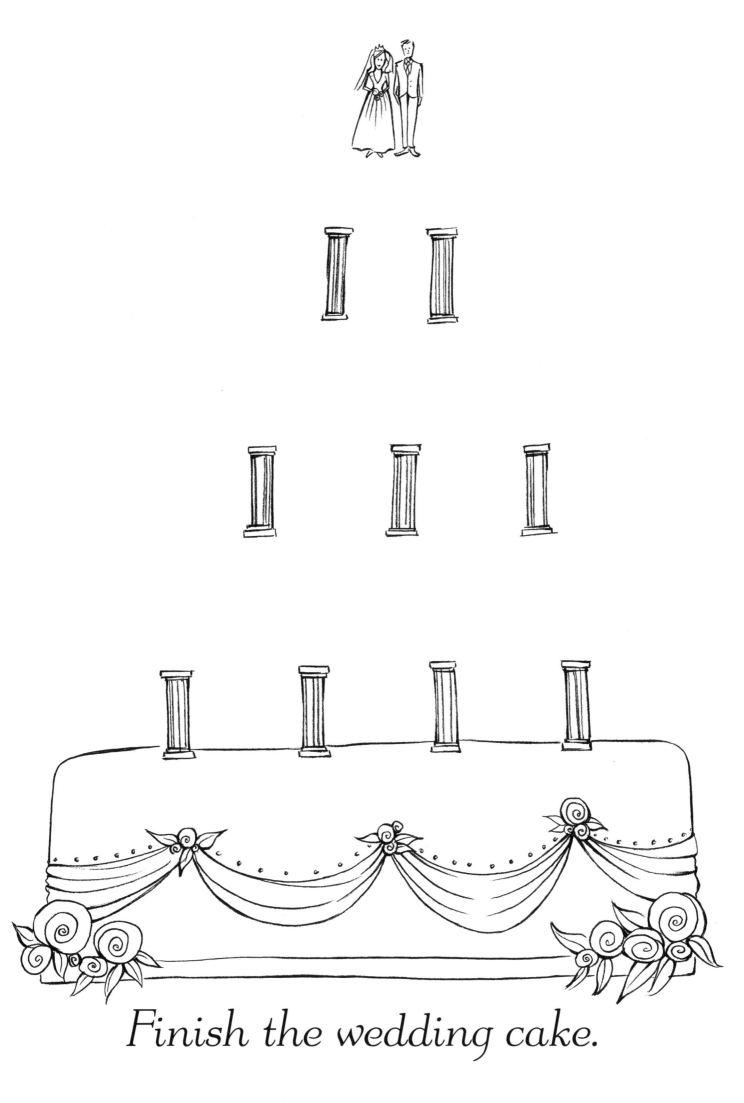

Finish the wedding cake.

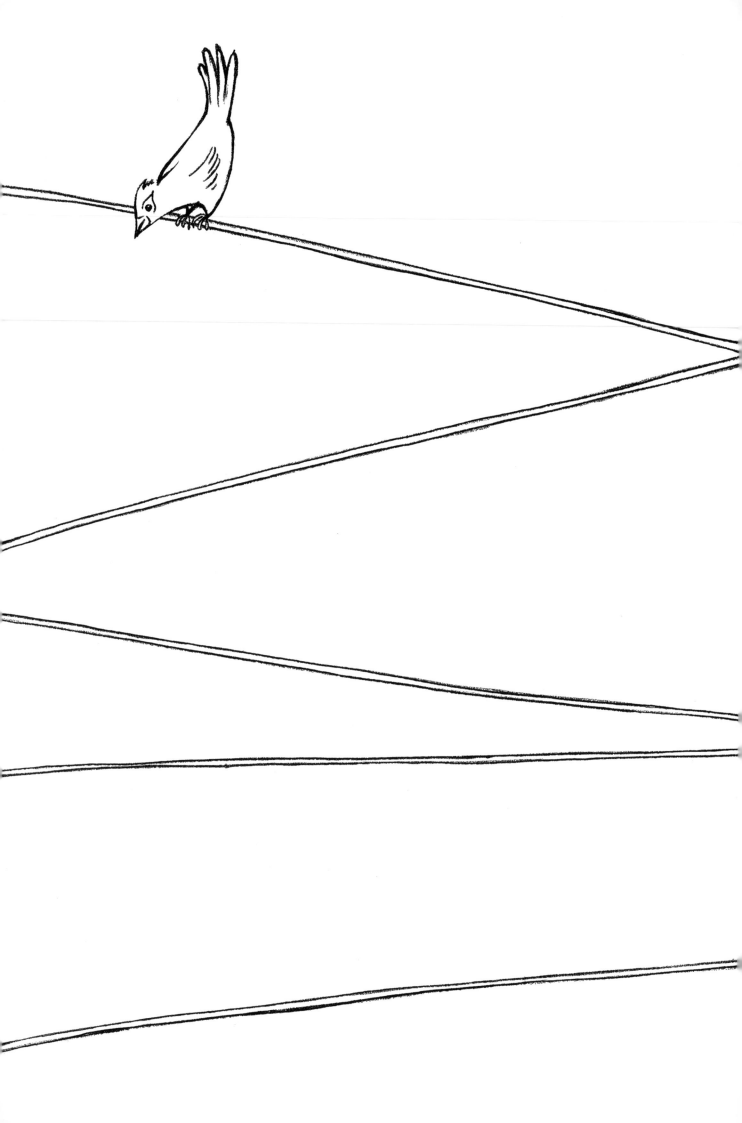

Put some birds on the lines.

So many delicious cakes!

Make a strawberry sundae.

Fill the shelves, and your trolley.

What is under the table?

Decorate the roller skates.

What can you see through the magic keyhole?

Design some magic keys.

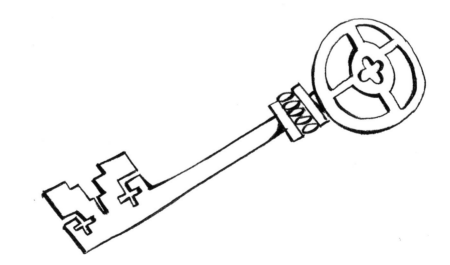

Catch it!

Make an exotic drink.

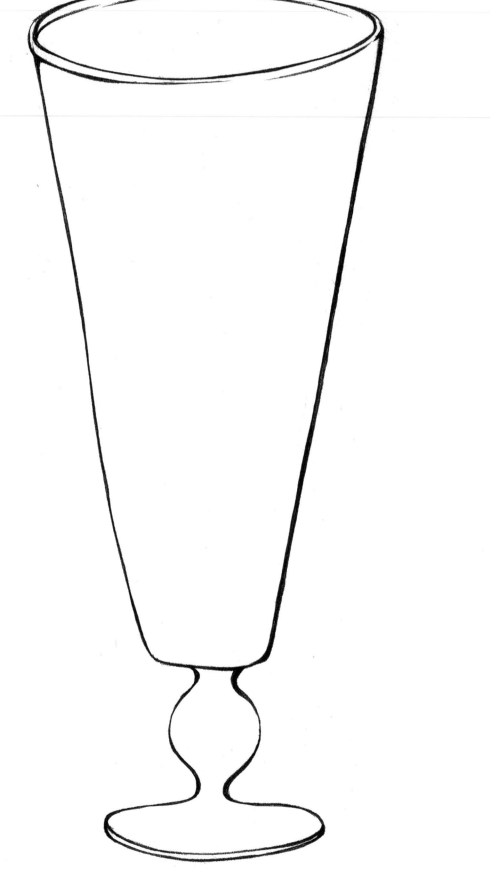

What is on the dressing table?

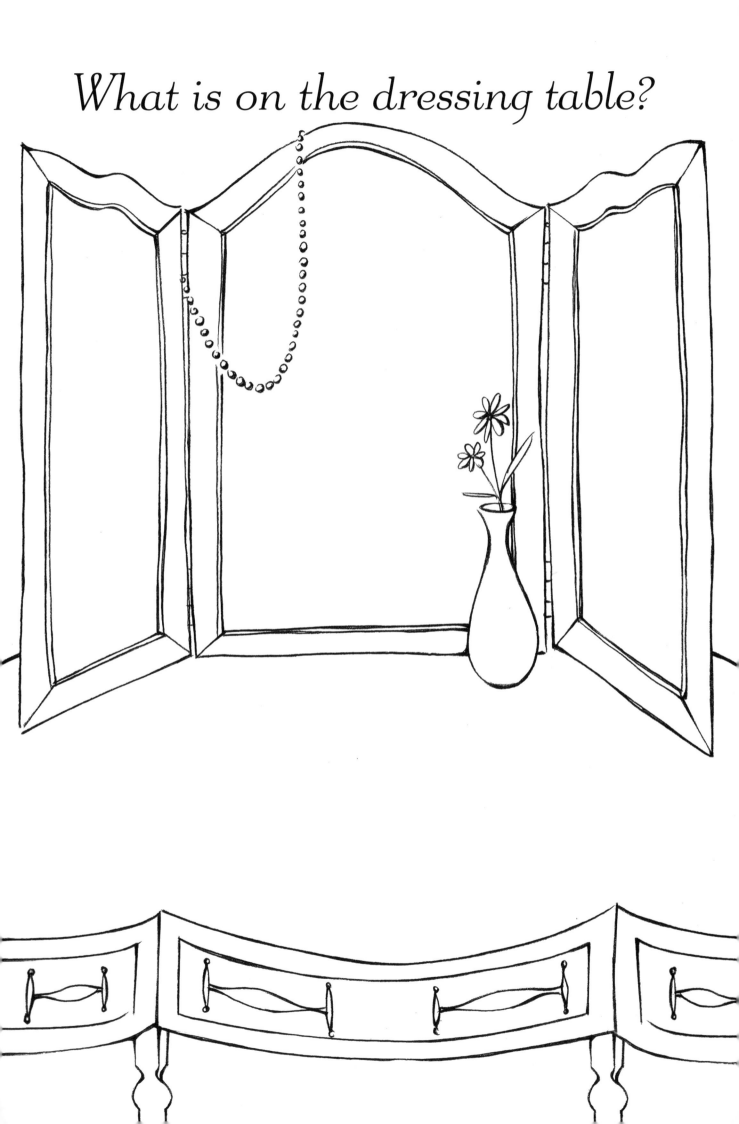

Paint patterns on the plates.

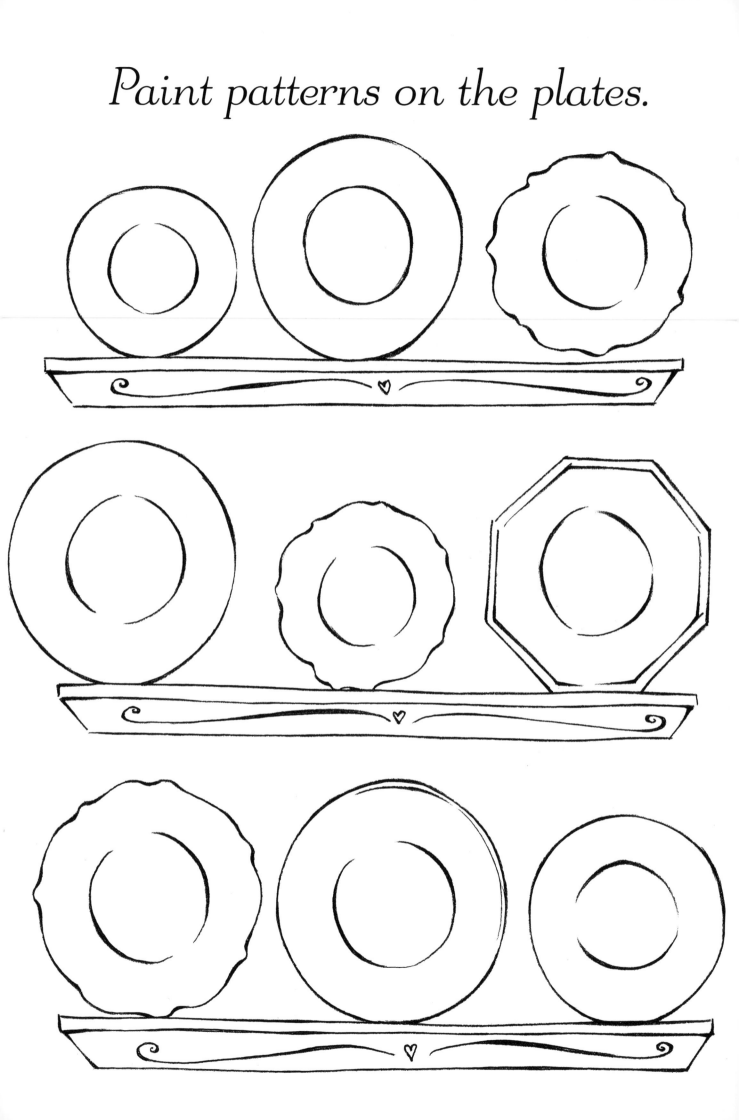

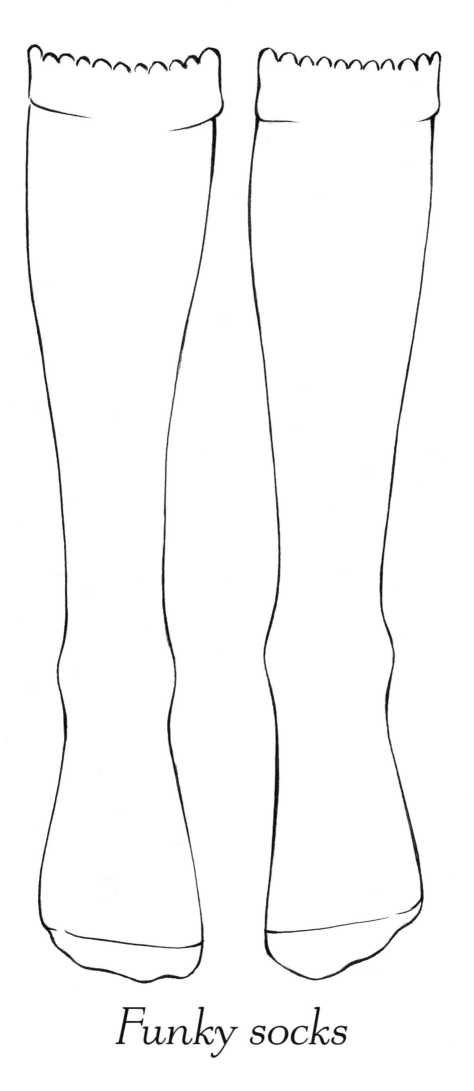

Funky socks

What is in the rock pools?

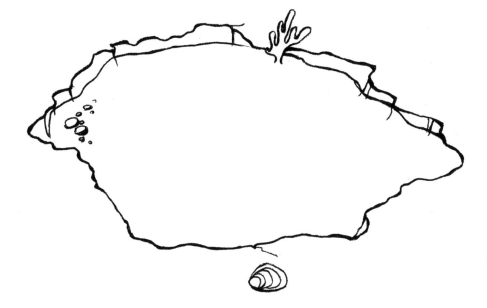
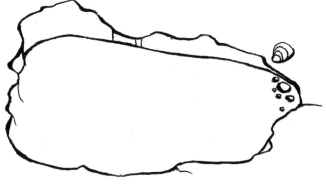
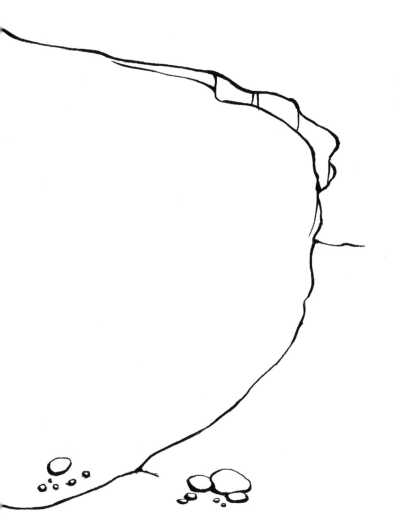

What is on the computer screen?

*Design a necklace for
each of your friends.*

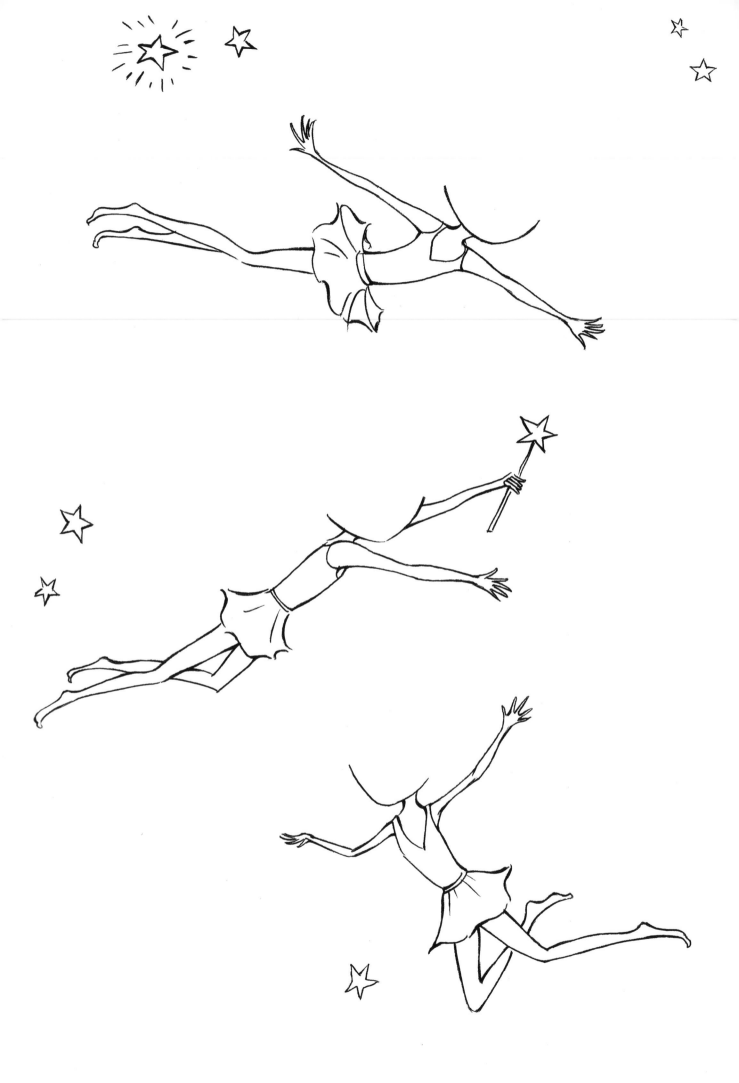

Finish the fairies and
give them wings.

The latest catwalk fashion.

*What is at the end of
the rainbow?*

Decorate the tea set.

A beautiful mermaid.

What does the baby need?

Design a card.

What can you see from the plane?

What a beautiful ball gown!

What kind of statue is on the plinth?

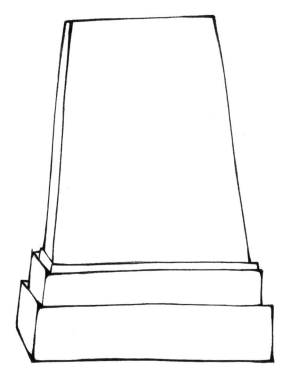

Pillow fight!

What are you knitting?

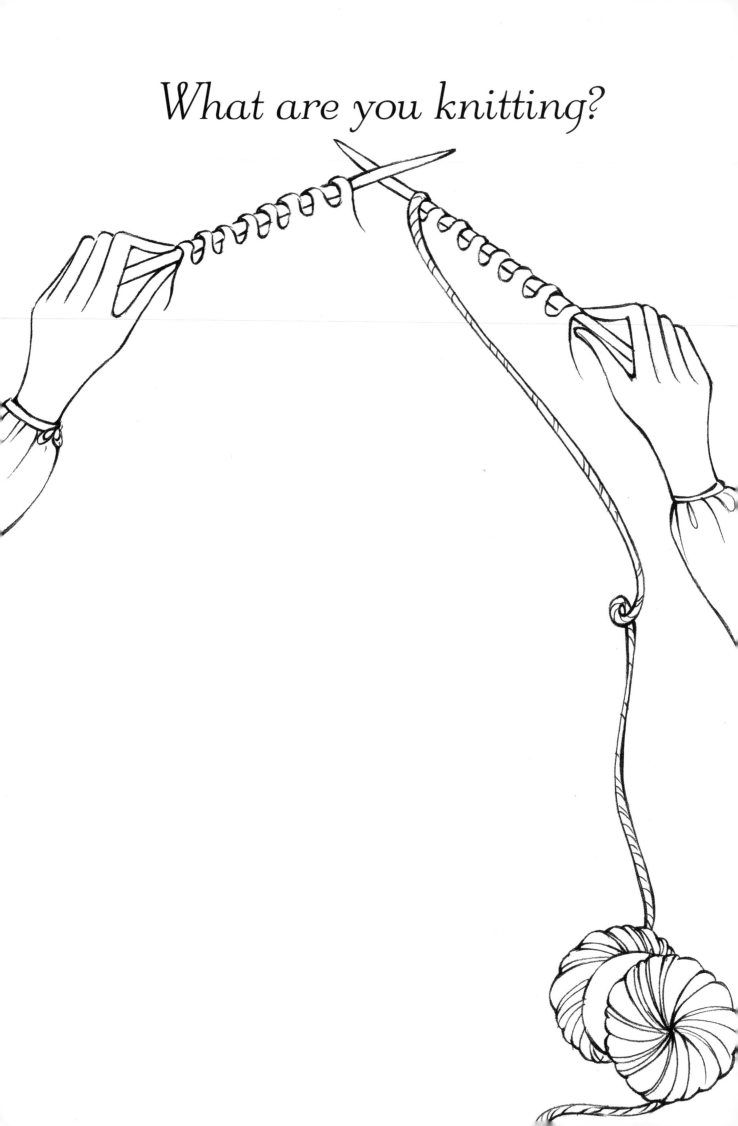

Design some fabulous earrings.

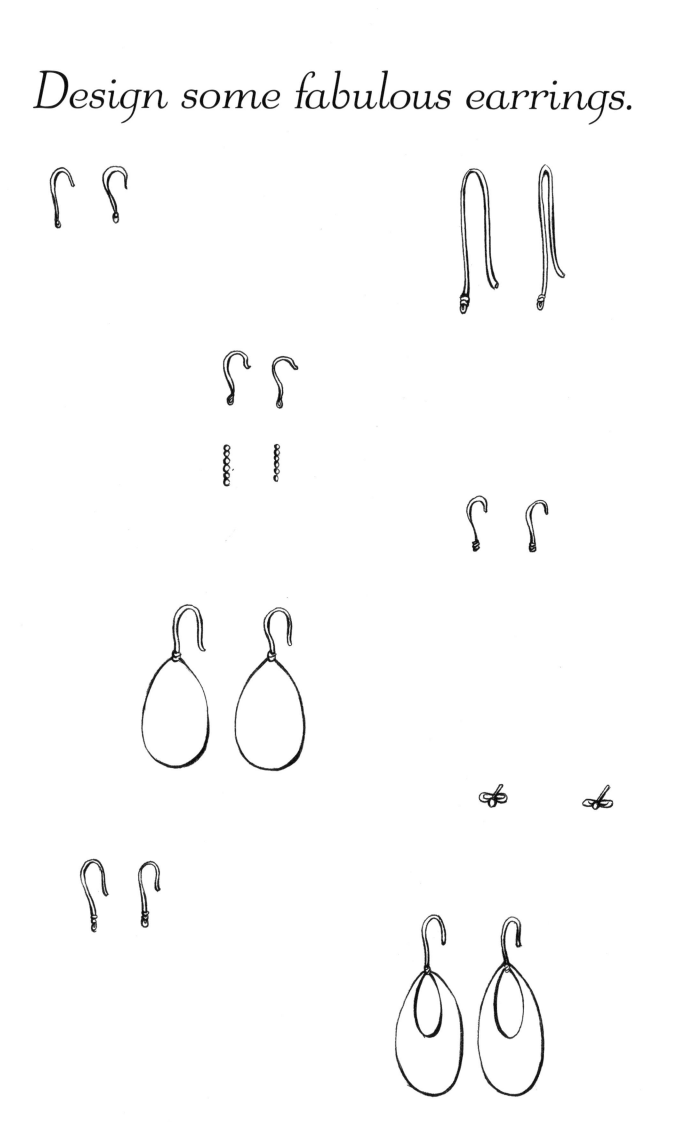

Design the book covers and fill the shelves.

Fill the bagel.

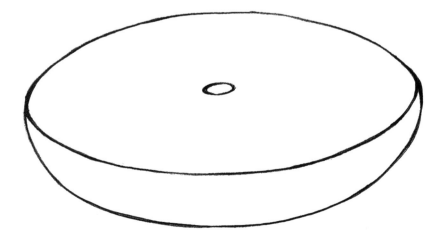

Design some cool album covers.

Mirror, mirror, on the wall . . .

What shapes are the balloons?

Let's go and fly a kite!

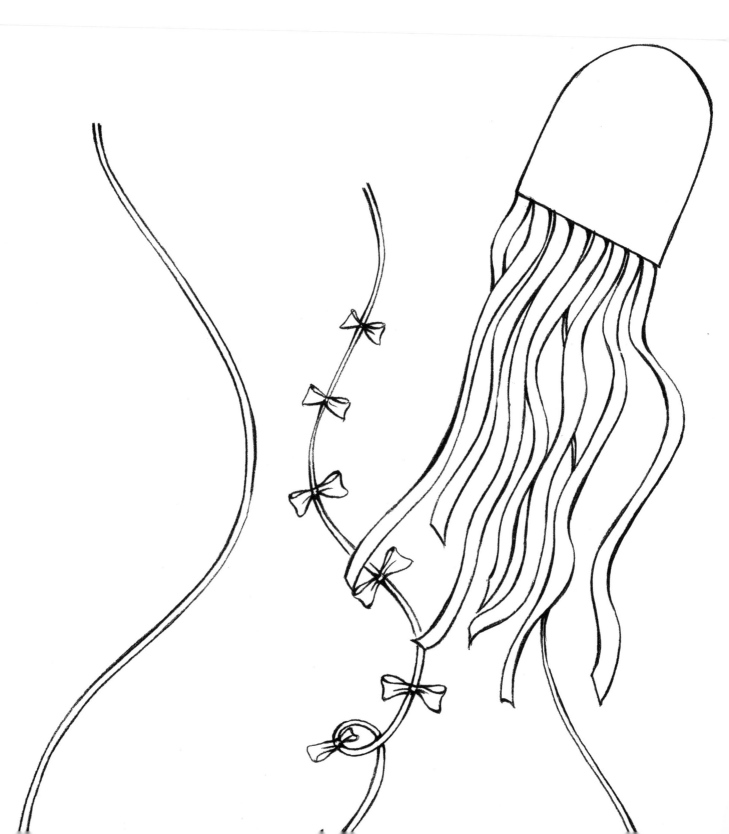

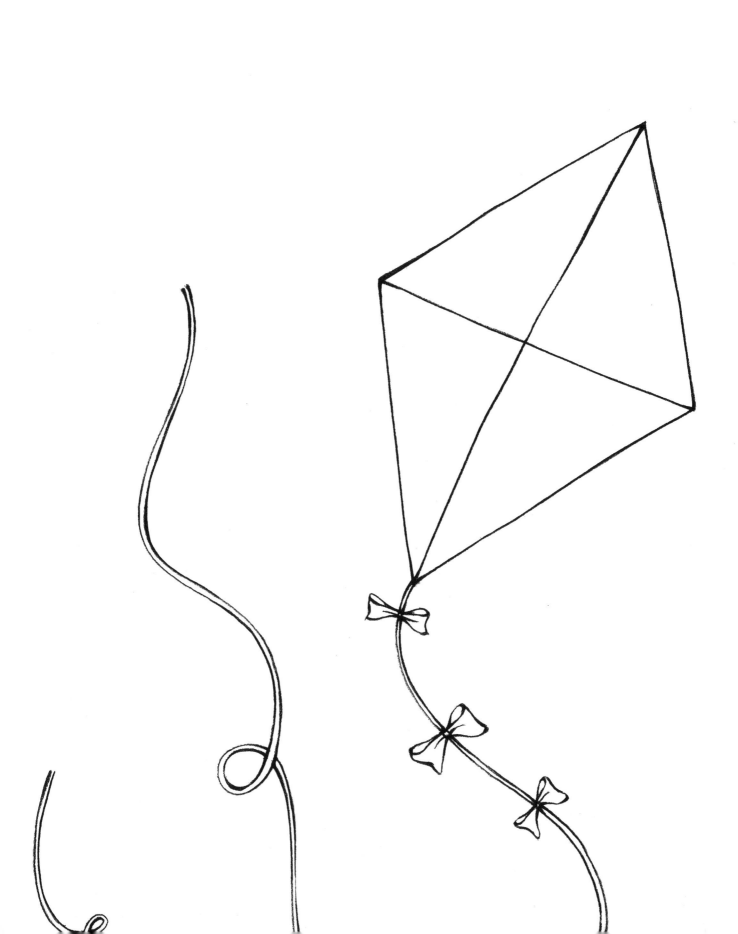

Finish the ballerina.

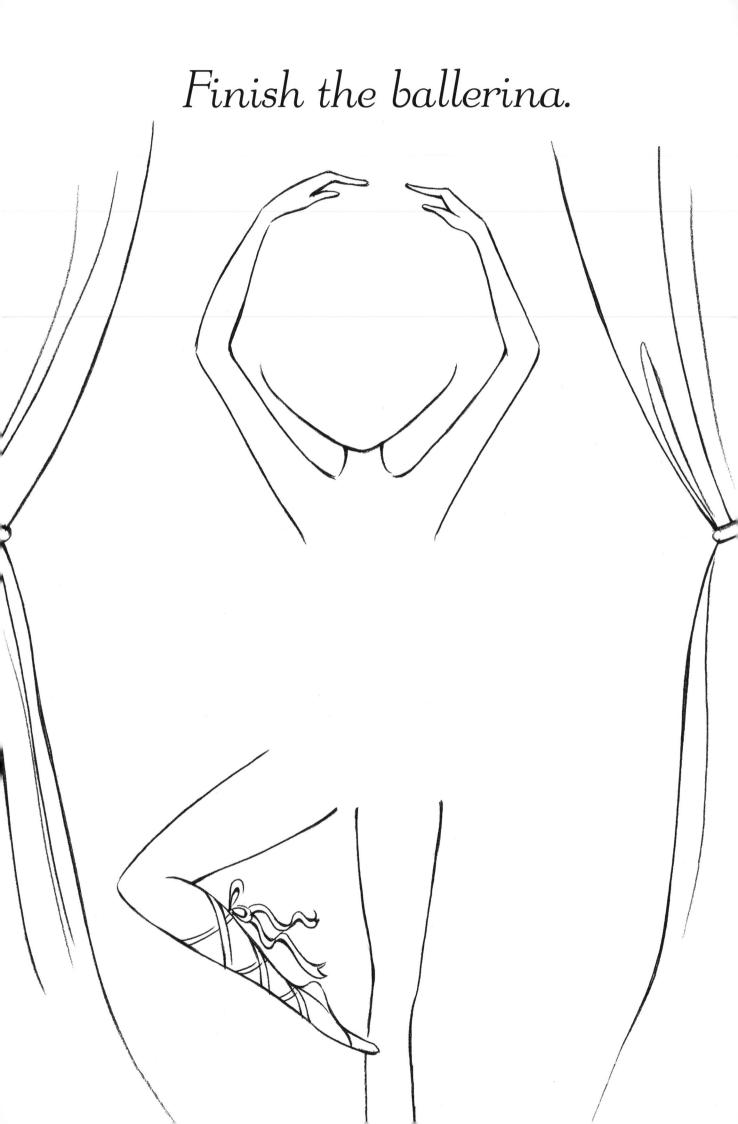

Decorate the wallpaper.

Make the rings sparkle.

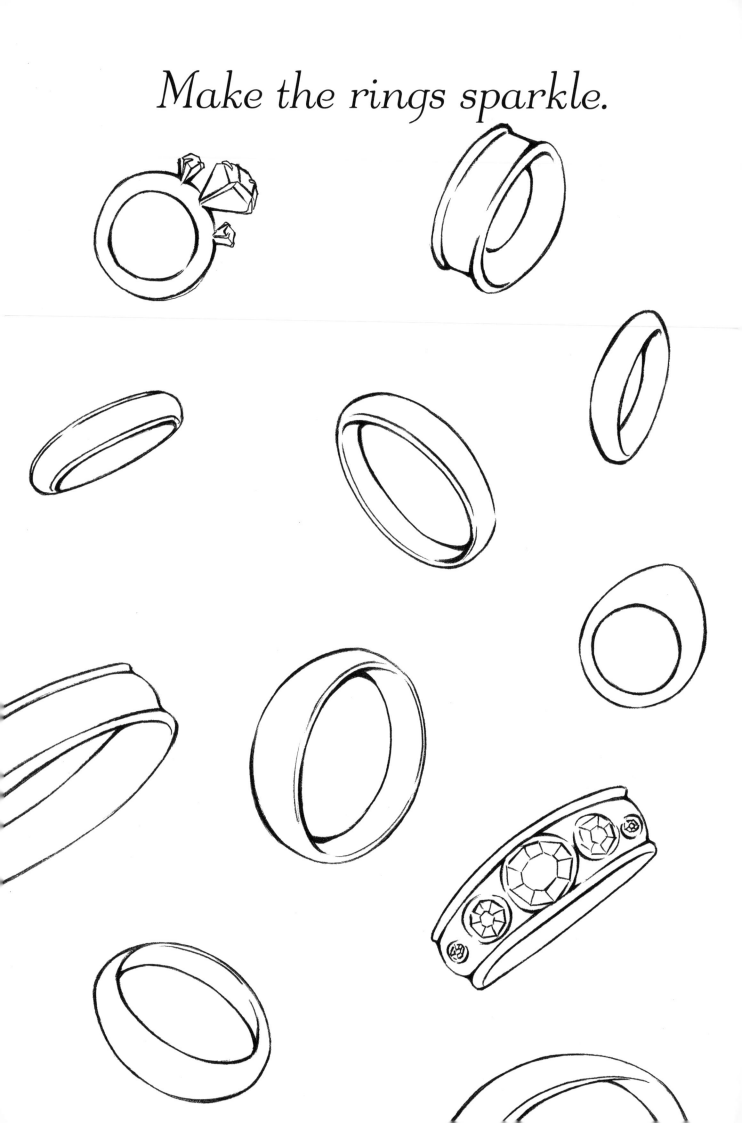

Walk your dogs.

Add lucky charms to the bracelet.

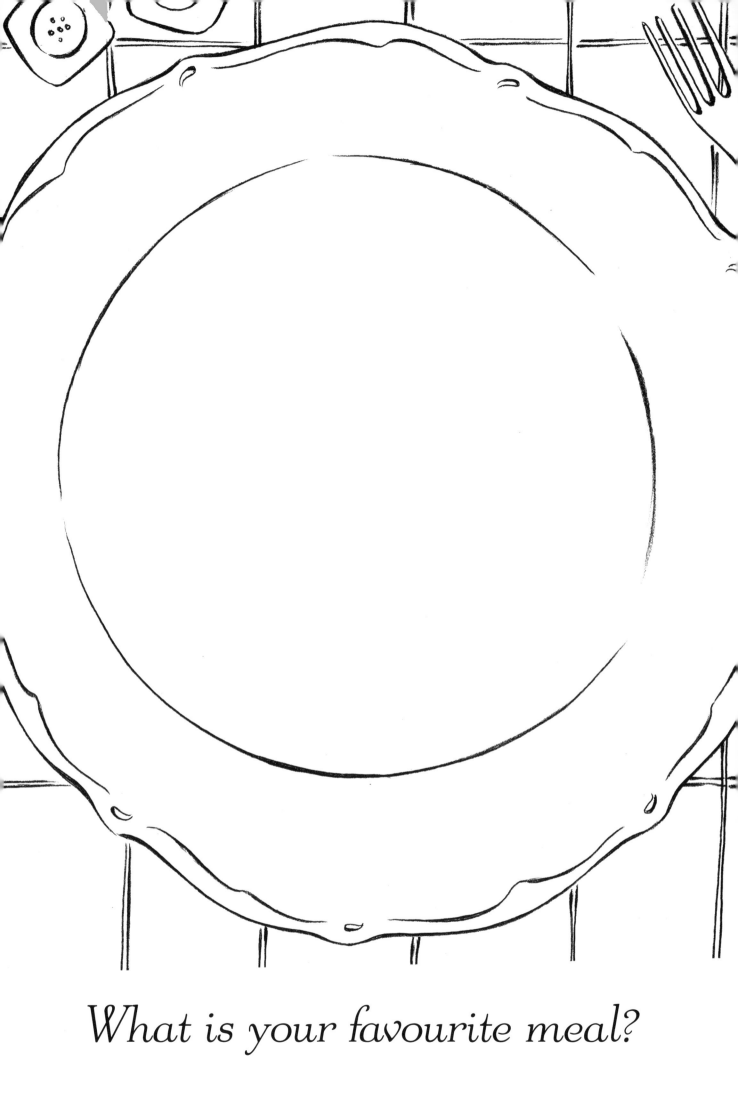

What is your favourite meal?

Design some handbags.

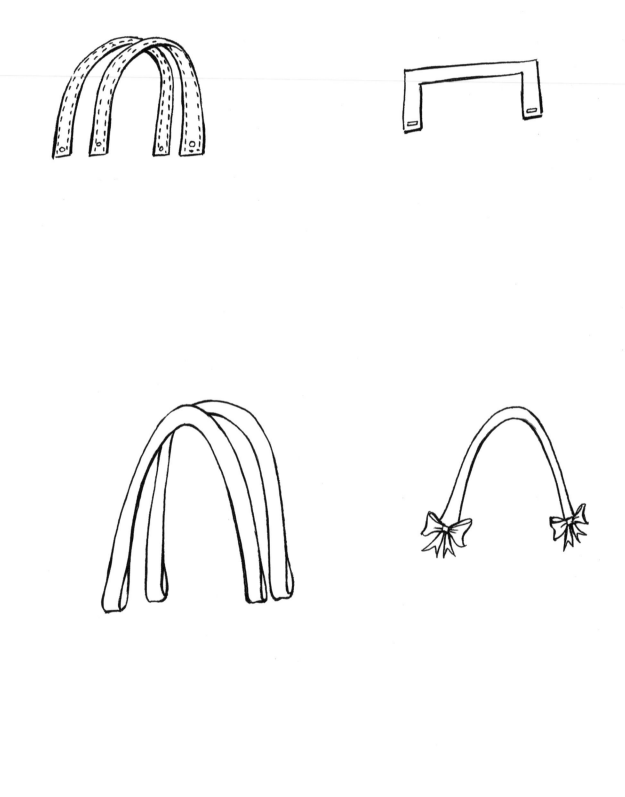

What ingredients are in your favourite smoothie?

What are the teddy bears having
for their picnic?

The perfect ice cream.

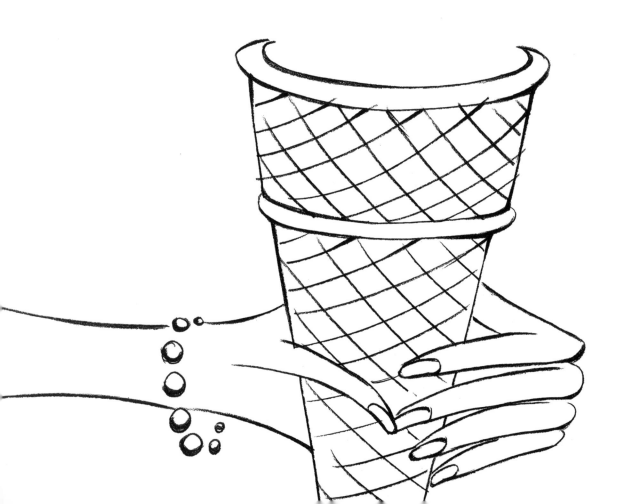

What can you see from
your hiding place?

What is in the refrigerator?

What do you need at the beach?

Where have you landed?

What is for afternoon tea?

Decorate the umbrellas.

What can you see at the aquarium?

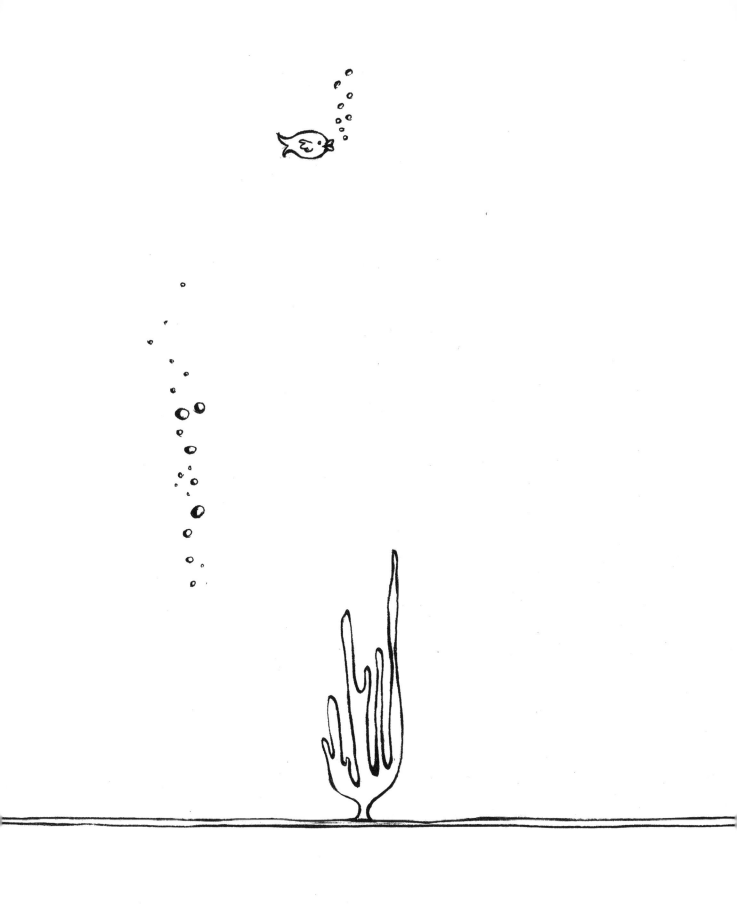

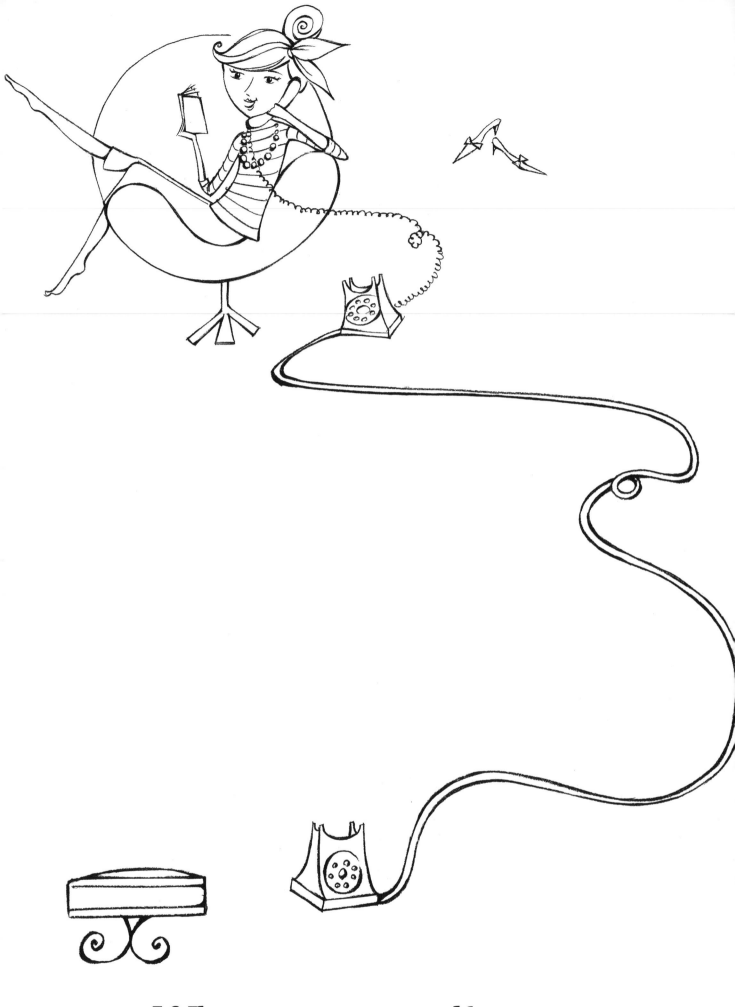

Who are you talking to?

So many sweets!

What can you pick from the tree?

Design a T-shirt.

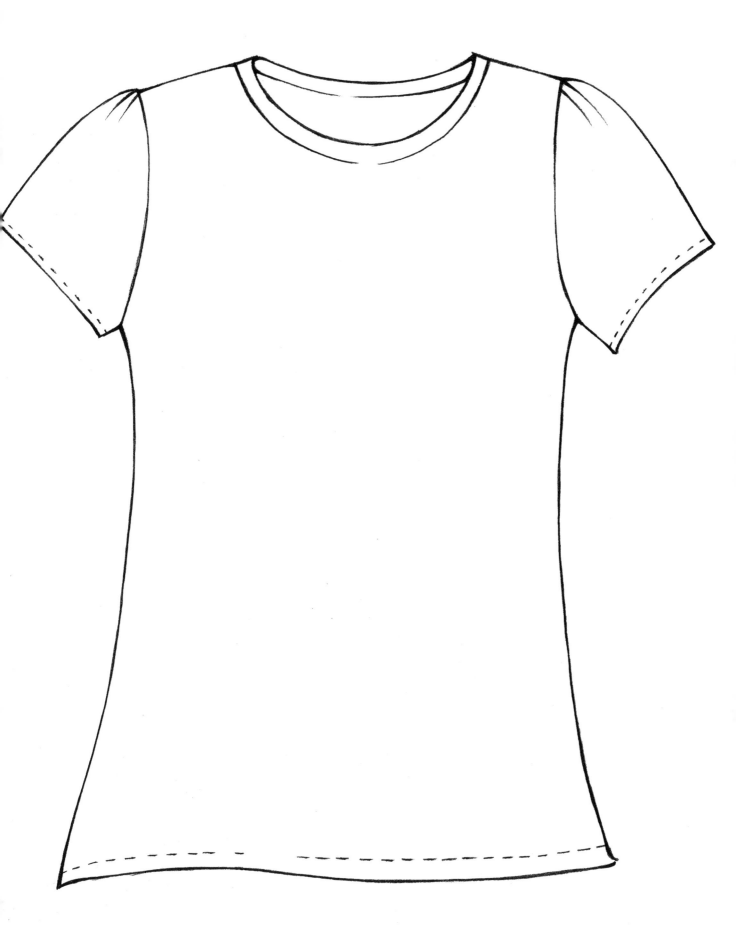

Twinkle, twinkle little stars!

What is being performed?

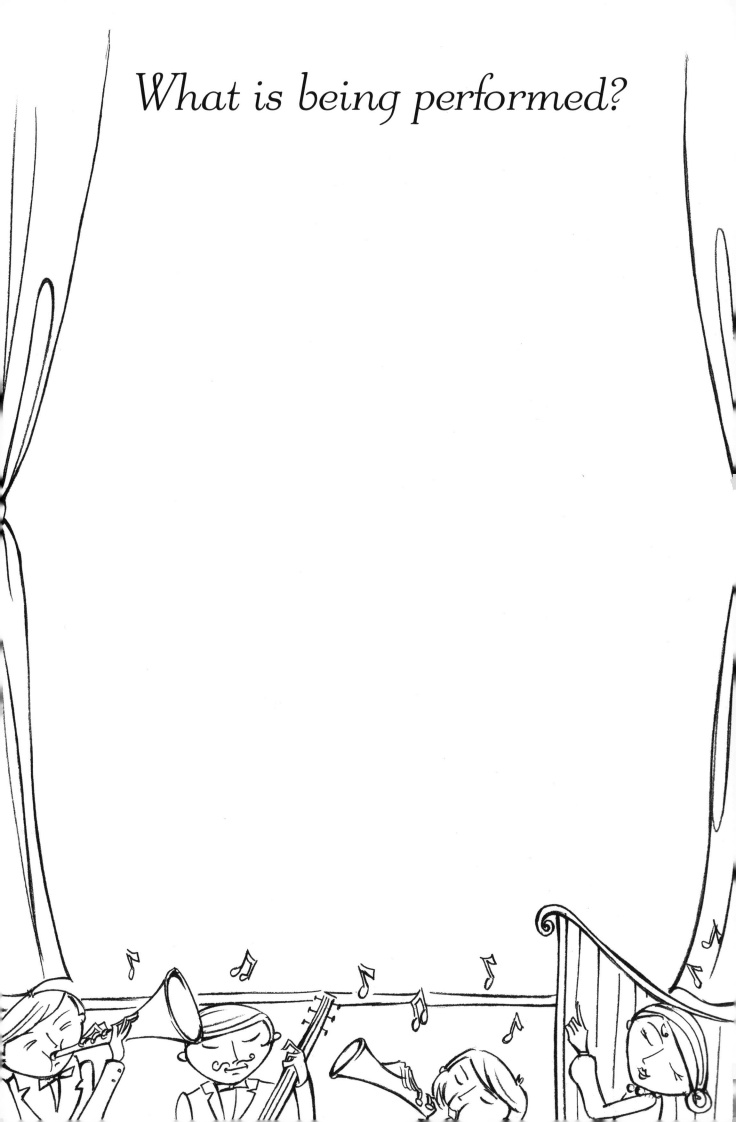

Where are these postcards from?

The best snowman ever.

Dress the shop windows.

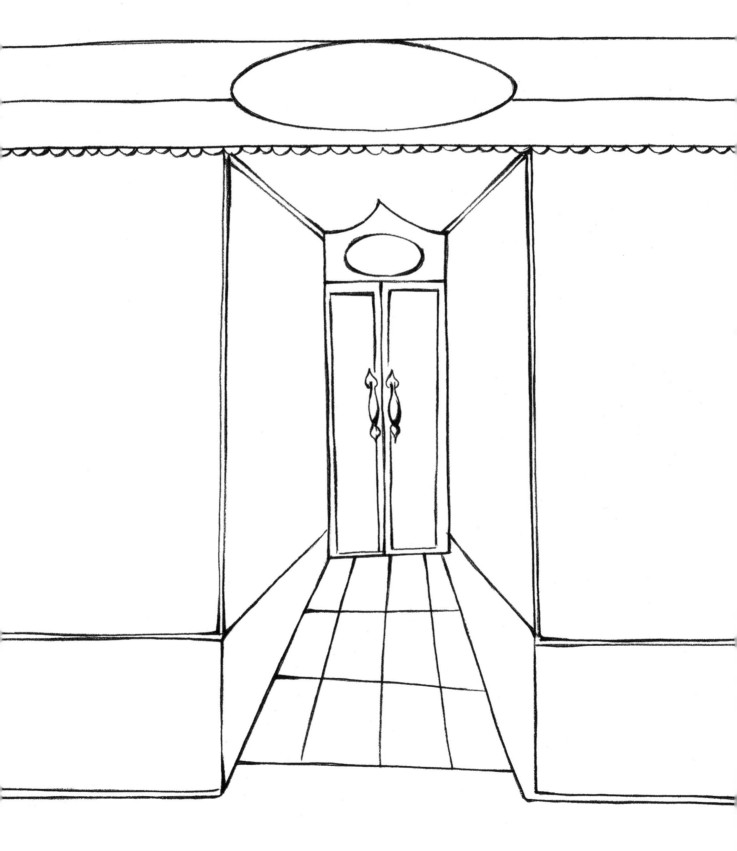

Lots of love.

Finish the Hawaiian necklace.

Design some flip-flops.

What is under the sea?

The secret garden.

Decorate the eggs.

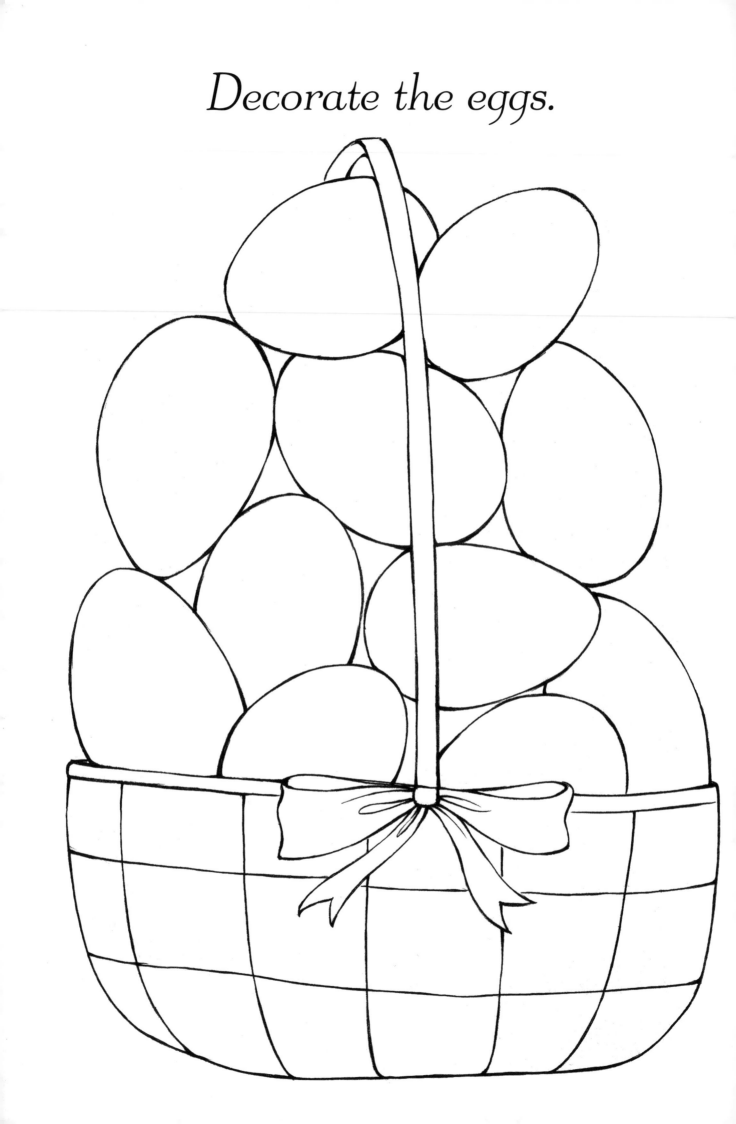

What have you unwrapped?

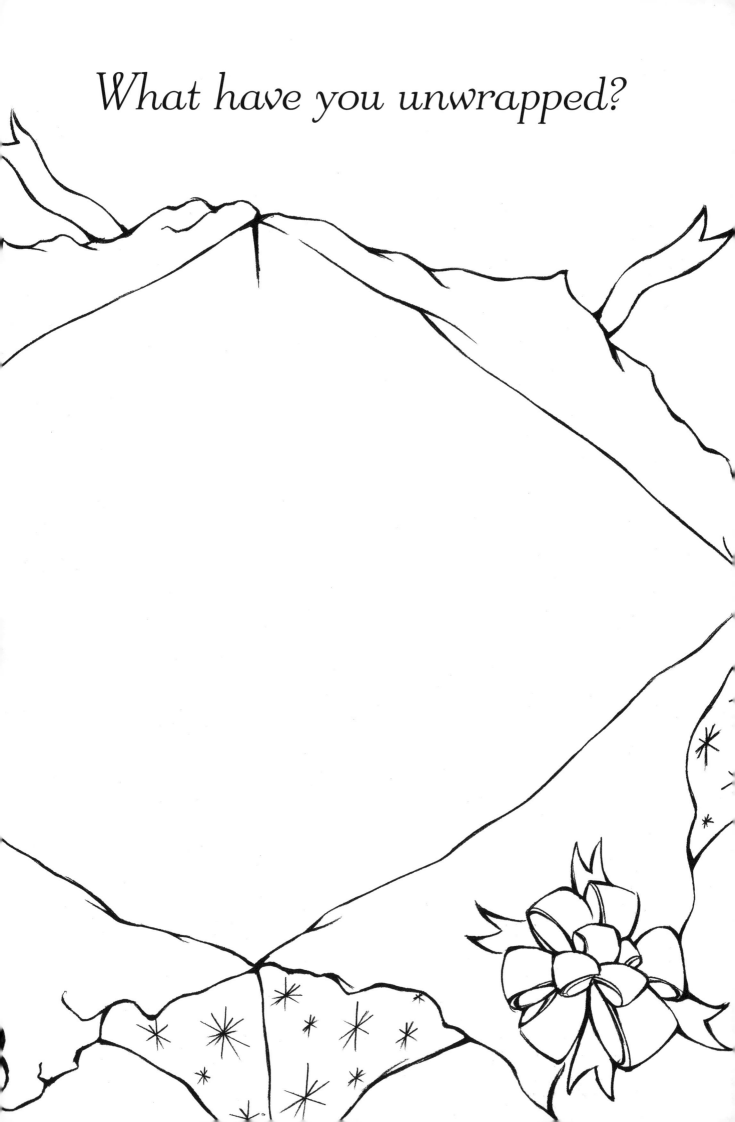

Ta-da!